THE MISSISSIPPI MUSICIANS

A RETELLING OF THE BREMEN TOWN MUSICIANS

STORY BY LESLIE FALCONER   PICTURES BY CHRIS LENSCH

First published by Experience Early Learning Company
7243 Scotchwood Lane, Grawn, Michigan 49637 USA

ISBN: 978-1-937954-29-1
Visit us at www.ExperienceEarlyLearning.com

Once upon a time there was a man who owned a donkey. The donkey carried sacks of grain to the mill for many years.

On his way back to the farm from the mill, the donkey would carry little children. The children would laugh and hug the donkey.

2

But the donkey was old now. He could no longer carry the heavy bags of grain.

"What is wrong with you?" the farmer shouted. "You are old and worthless."

The donkey was sad.
He loved helping and
knew he still had
talents to share.

5

The donkey decided, perhaps it was time that he follow his dream of playing the bass in a blues band. So the donkey ran away, and he headed for the Mississippi River.

Being in no hurry, the donkey walked slowly. When he arrived on the top of a big grassy hill, he heard a loud and lonesome howl.

8

A lonely looking dog was sitting in the road.
"Why are you crying, old fellow?" asked the donkey.
"When I was young I could chase the fastest birds,"
said the dog. "But now I am slow. The hunter said
I am old and worthless."

9

"But you have such a deep and soulful voice!" the donkey said. "Let's start a blues band! You can sing out your sadness and play the harmonica."

And so the dog joined the donkey.
They walked side by side down the
road to the Mississippi River.

As they walked through some tall, thick trees, they saw two big eyes staring down at them from the branches. "Hello? Who is up there?" the donkey asked. "Don't be scared. We won't hurt you."

A cat crept onto the branch above them. "I don't know what to do," meowed the cat quietly. "I am getting old, my teeth are dull, and I can no longer chase mice. The seamstress said I am old and worthless. She doesn't even give me string to play with anymore." The cat cried a melancholy meow.

"Join our blues band!" exclaimed the donkey. "You can pluck out your sadness on the strings of a guitar."

And so the cat jumped out of the tree and pranced down the road to the Mississippi River with the donkey and the dog.

The animals walked
for miles. Then, as
the sun was about
to set, a chicken
came running
towards them in
a fright.

16

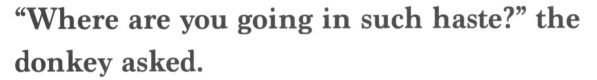

"Where are you going in such haste?" the donkey asked.

"I don't know, but I must go fast," clucked the chicken. "The cook said I was old and worthless because I no longer lay eggs. If I don't run, I will surely become Sunday's soup." The chicken pecked the ground in a steady, nervous beat.

"But you have talent!" declared the donkey. "Join our blues band! You can beat back your worries while you play the drums.

18

And so the chicken clucked and strutted down the road to the Mississippi River with the donkey, the dog and the cat.

19

As evening approached, they finally reached the banks of the Mississippi River. They were very tired from their long journey. The donkey and the dog lay down beneath a big tree, the cat climbed up onto a branch and the chicken sat upon a pile of leaves. However, they did not feel safe.

The chicken looked around in all directions and noticed a faint light in the distance. "Look! A light!" she said. "Perhaps we'll find a place to stay."

The dog jumped up first.

Together they set off toward the light. It grew brighter and brighter. When they found themselves outside a cozy cabin the donkey, being the tallest, went to the window and peeked inside.

"What do you see?" asked the others.
"I see a warm fire, a table full of delicious food and three thieves holding forks and knives!" replied the donkey.

The animals were old, but they were very wise. They devised a sneaky plan. The donkey stood strong. The dog jumped onto the donkey's back. The cat climbed on top of the dog. And the chicken perched upon the cat's head.

Once in position the donkey pushed open the door and they began to make a ruckus! The donkey brayed, the dog barked, the cat meowed and the chicken clucked. The terrified thieves looked at the great beast with its eight eyes and winged head. It made such a horrible noise!

CLUCK

MEOW MEOW

HEHAW

WOOF

OO

29

The thieves tumbled through the
nearest window and fled forever
into the darkness.

Each of the animals ate a delicious treat and dozed off in the warmth and safety of the cabin.

The very next morning in their small cabin on the edge of the Mississippi River, they strummed, hummed and drummed the blues.

Now, whenever someone is sad and doesn't know where to go, they can follow the music to the Mississippi River and sing away their blues.